CW00549469

DON BOSCO PUBLICATIONS

Kathleen Pearce

Katie
Comes to Mass

Illustrations by Martina Špinková

DON BOSCO PUBLICATIONS

It had been a long hot summer. Now the days were getting a little cooler and the school holidays were coming to an end. Rosie's cousin, Katie, was staying for a few days; tomorrow she would be going home. It was Sunday and Rosie was determined to enjoy their last day together. First they were going to Mass and afterwards, they planned to have a family picnic. Katie had not been to Mass before and Rosie was looking forward to quietly telling Katie all that happens during the service.

They left home early in order to find a seat close to the front, but as they entered the church they noticed it was already quite full.

osie dipped the tips of her fingers in the holy water and made the sign of the cross. Katie watched carefully, then she too blessed herself, and followed Rosie quietly down the aisle, where they both genuflected before sitting in the pew close to the altar.

Katie looked around the church. It was beautiful. There were candles burning brightly on the altar and the church was decorated with pink and white flowers. Everyone was very quiet; some were kneeling down saying their prayers, and others were reading their prayer books.

Suddenly Katie heard a little bell ring, and Rosie told her it meant that Mass was about to start. The organ began to play and everyone stood up and started to sing as the priest and altar servers walked to the altar.

The Mass begins

The priest stood in front of the altar and said, ***In the name of the Father, and of the Son, and of the Holy Spirit.*** The congregation joined in and they all made the sign of the cross. The priest welcomed everyone to Mass, and said, ***The Lord be with you***. Everyone answered, ***And with your spirit***.

Asking Forgiveness

The priest then asked everyone to think about their sins. He asked them to say sorry to God and to each other for what they had done wrong. Katie quietly asked Rosie why they had to ask each other for forgiveness, as well as asking God. Rosie told her that sometimes people are not nice to each other, and upset each other. *Do you remember when we argued the other day, and then said sorry and were friends again? It's good to say sorry and ask each other for forgiveness.*

The priest made the sign of the cross and said, **May almighty God have mercy on us, forgive us our sins, and bring us to everlasting life.**

The Gloria

The people all prayed together,
praising God saying,
Glory to God in the Highest, and on earth
peace to people of good will. We praise you,
we bless you, we adore you, we glorify you,
we give you thanks for your great glory, Lord
God, heavenly King, O God, almighty Father.
Rosie whispered to Katie.
This prayer is called the Gloria,
it's a happy prayer.

The First Reading

Shortly afterwards everyone sat down, and a woman in the congregation went up to the lectern and read from the Old Testament. She announced that the first reading was from the prophet Isaiah. When she finished reading, she said, *The word of the Lord.* Everyone answered, *Thanks be to God.* Katie asked Rosie, *What's a prophet?* Rosie whispered to her, *A prophet is a holy and wise man who tells us about God.*

The Second Reading

This reading was from the New Testament and was from a letter St Paul wrote to the Romans. When the reader had finished she said, **The word of the Lord.** Katie answered in a rather loud voice, **Thanks be to God.** Rosie smiled. Katie was really beginning to feel part of the Mass. *Why did St Paul write to the Romans?* asked Katie. Rosie replied, *Paul wanted to tell people about Jesus. He wanted them to know about God.*

The Gospel

Everyone in church stood up and began to say a prayer called the **Alleluia**. Katie noticed that the priest was now walking towards the lectern. *The priest is going to read the gospel,* whispered Rosie. ***The Lord be with you,*** said the priest and the people answered, ***And with your spirit.***

The priest then told everyone that today's gospel was according to St Matthew.

Rosie told Katie that the gospels were stories from the life of Jesus. The word gospel meant good news. The gospels were written by the four evangelists, Matthew, Mark, Luke and John.

The Homily

Today the gospel was about one of the many times Jesus spoke to the crowds who followed him. Jesus told them about God, and used stories to help them to understand. When the priest had finished reading the gospel, he said, ***The Gospel of the Lord.***

Everyone answered, ***Praise to you, Lord Jesus Christ.***

The people then sat down and the priest began speaking about all he had read in the Gospel. Rosie and Katie listened carefully.

The Creed

When the priest had finished speaking, everyone stood up and started to say The Creed.
Rosie handed Katie her prayer book and they read it together.

I believe in God, the Father almighty,
Creator of heaven and earth,
and in Jesus Christ, his only Son, our Lord,
> (During the reading of the next two lines, everyone bowed their heads.)

who was conceived by the Holy Spirit,
born of the Virgin Mary, suffered under Pontius Pilate,
was crucified, died and was buried;
he descended into hell; on the third day he rose again
from the dead; he ascended into heaven,
and is seated at the right hand of God the Father
almighty; from there he will come to judge the living
and the dead.
I believe in the Holy Spirit, the holy catholic Church,
the communion of saints, the forgiveness of sins,
the resurrection of the body, and life everlasting.
Amen.

21

The Bidding Prayers

When everyone had finished saying The Creed, the reader went up to the lectern once more. Rosie told Katie that it was now time for the bidding prayers, when we ask God for special blessings on people.

Prayers were also asked for people in other parts of the world, especially those who were poor, suffering, or persecuted. At the end of each prayer the reader said, *Lord hear us,* and everyone answered, *Lord graciously hear us.*

The Offertory

K atie watched as the priest took the bread and wine from the servers.

Now we are getting ready for the most sacred part of the Mass, Rosie whispered. *This is the time when we remember the last meal Jesus had with his friends.* Katie asked, *Was that called the last supper?* Rosie nodded, and said, *The priest will now take the bread and the wine and bless them.*

They both listened carefully as the priest first blessed the bread and then the wine. After each blessing, everyone in the church said, **Blessed be God forever.**

Katie thought about the bread, and how it grows from a little seed and is ripened by the sun. She realised that this was very special bread. It will become the body of Christ.

The wine, which had started as little seedlings and produced grapes from its beautiful vines, will become the blood of Christ.

The Collection

Now it was time for the collection. Rosie and Katie opened their purses and put the money Rosie's Mummy had given them into the collection baskets. Rosie knew that this offering would be used by the priest to buy things for the church. It would also go towards helping those in need, such as children, and the elderly or poor, also the homeless.

The priest started to speak once more, *Pray, brothers and sisters, that my sacrifice and yours may be acceptable to God, the almighty Father.* The people rose and replied:
May the Lord accept the sacrifice at your hands for the praise and glory of his name, for our good and the good of all his holy Church.

The Eucharistic Prayer

The priest then started to say the Eucharistic Prayer which is the most important part of the Mass. He praised God and thanked him for sending his son Jesus to us. The people then joined in and said, *Holy, Holy, Holy Lord God of hosts. Heaven and earth are full of your glory. Hosanna in the highest. Blessed is he who comes in the name of the Lord. Hosanna in the highest.* Everyone knelt down.

The priest continued with the Eucharistic Prayer, remembering the Last Supper when Jesus told his apostles that although it was their last meal together, he would always be with them.

The priest held up the host and said, *Take this, all of you, and eat of it, for this is my body which will be given up for you.* He then lifted the chalice and said, *Take this, all of you, and drink from it: for this is the chalice of my Blood, the Blood of the new and eternal covenant, which will be poured out for you and for many for the forgiveness of sins. Do this in memory of me.* The bread and wine had now become the body and blood of Jesus.

35

Our Father

The priest said, ***Let us pray.*** Everyone stood up. Rosie told Katie they were now going to say **The Our Father.** Katie was pleased because she had learnt this prayer at school, and she could now join in. It was good to hear everyone praying together, *Our Father, who art in heaven, hallowed be thy name; thy kingdom come, thy will be done on earth as it is in heaven. Give us this day our daily bread, and forgive us our trespasses, as we forgive those who trespass against us; and lead us not into temptation, but deliver us from evil.*

The Sign of Peace

The priest said, ***The peace of the Lord be with you always.*** Everyone replied, ***And with your spirit.*** The priest then said, ***Let us offer each other the sign of peace.*** Rosie and Katie shook hands with each other and the people around them.

The priest then broke the bread and lifted it up. He said, *Behold the Lamb of God, behold him who takes away the sins of the world. Blessed are those called to the supper of the Lamb.* The people replied, *Lord, I am not worthy that you should enter under my roof, but only say the word and my soul shall be healed.*

Holy Communion

It was now time for Holy Communion. Katie followed Rosie up to the altar, and watched as Rosie received Communion. Katie had not made her First Communion so she crossed her arms to let the priest know she would like a blessing. Gently the priest made the sign of the cross on Katie's head and blessed her.

They returned to their seats and Rosie knelt down to pray. Katie looked around the church, the people next to her were praying too. She didn't know many prayers but she knew that it was a time when she could just speak to God in her own words. She sat quietly and asked God to look after her family. She thanked God for the blessing she had just received. It was a very special moment.

When everyone had received Holy Communion, the priest returned to the altar and started to clean the chalice and the paten. He put the remaining communion hosts into a very special container called a ciborium and put them safely into the tabernacle. Katie noticed a little red lamp burning next to the tabernacle. *Why is that lamp red Rosie? Why is it different from all the other candles on the altar?* In reply Rosie whispered, *It's called the sanctuary lamp, it lets people know that the Blessed Sacrament is in the tabernacle.*

The Final Blessing

The Mass was nearing the end now, but first the priest read the church notices. He reminded everyone of the times of the services during the coming week, and the names of those who were ill. He also reminded the parents that the children would be returning to school the following week, and he wished them all well. Rosie and Katie looked at each other and smiled. It had been a good holiday, but now they were ready for school again. The priest said, *The Lord be with you.* Everyone answered, *And with your spirit.* He said the final prayers and blessing. *May almighty God bless you: the Father, and the Son, and the Holy Spirit.* They all made the sign of the cross, and answered *Amen.*

Everyone sang the final hymn and then slowly left the church. Outside, people were talking in small groups and wishing each other a nice day. *I enjoyed the Mass, Rosie, can I come again?* said Katie. *Yes, and next time you will know what is happening during the service,* laughed Rosie, *and I won't have to keep whispering to you.* They were ready to go home now, and prepare for the last outing of the summer holidays. It was a beautiful day and Rosie's parents had packed a delicious picnic. Going to Mass had been the perfect start to what was going to be a perfect day.

Contents

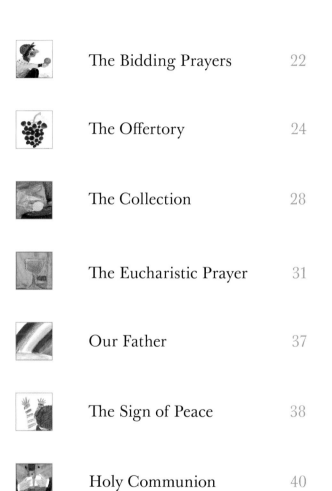

Other books by Kathleen Pearce

ROSIE GOES TO CHURCH
A child's guide to the church.

DVD ROSIE GOES TO CHURCH
A child's guide to the church in 9 languages.

GOOD NEWS IN THE FAMILY
The life of Jesus in story form.

OUR COLOURFUL CHURCH YEAR
The Church Year explained to children.

101 SAINTS AND SPECIAL PEOPLE
Lives of Saints for children.

CHLOE AND JACK VISIT THE VATICAN
A child's guide to the Vatican.

ISBN 978-0-955-56547-2

9 780955 565472 >

© Don Bosco Publications 2011
Thornleigh House
Sharples Park
Bolton
BL1 6PQ
England
Tel: 01204 308811
Email: joyce@salesians.org.uk
www.don-bosco-publications.co.uk